CW00540502

IRIS
folding
for Christmas

Maruscha Gaasenbeek
and Tine Beauveser

FORTE PUBLISHERS

Contents

Seventh printing September 2003
ISBN 90 5877 184 9

This is a publication from
Forte Publishers BV
P.O. Box 1394
3500 BJ Utrecht
The Netherlands

For more information about the
creative books available from
Forte Publishers:
www.hobby-party.com

Publisher: Marianne Perlot
Editor: Hanny Vlaar
Photography and digital image
editing: Fotografie Gerhard Witteveen,
Apeldoorn, the Netherlands
Cover and inner design:
Studio Herman Bade BV, Baarn,
the Netherlands

Preface

The new, original technique to make your own, beautiful greeting cards is called: IRIS folding. Special for the festive period we created IRIS Folding for Christmas with fifteen patterns. The work material is free, since you will find envelopes in your letterbox every day.

You cut them into strips and use the colours and patterns printed on the inside. You will be amazed by what you discover when you see the diversity of prints. Texts strips with the words Merry Christmas and a Happy New Year have been included with various cards specially for this book. Your good wishes will then be included in the design!

The narrow glitter borders for the Christmas ball, double star and champagne glasses make the cards look even more festive. Narrow gold or silver strips give a refined effect. It is a real challenge to apply these extra effects in various different ways!

A smaller version is given of a number of patterns, which can be used to make gift labels and bookmarkers. The first thing to do is to collect a good stock of envelopes! You can then start straight away, so that you can finish these original greetings cards in time for Christmas. Iris folding is an enjoyable and relaxing activity everybody can do. The drawing templates and punch cards make the work a bit easier. The patterns are not difficult to copy. But once you start, stopping will be difficult.

We wish you lots of fun with IRIS Folding for Christmas!

Maruscha   *Tine*

Thanks:
Marjolein, Francien, Ada, Joke, Roelof, Jannie, Henny, Hermien, Ina, José, Clarie, family and friends for all your enthusiasm and the pretty and constantly surprising work material.

Techniques

The starting point for iris folding is the pattern. Cut the outer shape of the pattern out of the card and then fill the hole from the outside to the inside with folded strips of used envelopes to which you add strips of text. You work at the back of your card, so that you work, in fact, on a mirror image, and when you have finished, you stick it onto another card.

For a square pattern, select four different envelopes where the patterns and colours combine and contrast each other nicely. Cut all the envelopes into strips in the same way, for example, from left to right. The number of strips you will need depends on the pattern; you will need between four and eight strips. The width of the strips also depends on the pattern and is given for each card. You need to first fold the edge of the strips over and sort them into each different type of envelope. Next, you cover each section in turn by following the numbers (1, 2, 3, 4, 5, etc.), so that you rotate the pattern. Lay the strips with the fold facing towards the middle of the pattern and then stick them on the left-hand and right-hand sides of the card using adhesive tape. Finally, stick on an attractive piece of holographic paper to cover the hole in the middle. Avoid colour differences by using one envelope for the same design.

The BASIC SQUARE
(see card 3 in chapter 1)

The most important thing is to start with the basic square, because from this, you will learn the unique folding and sticking technique needed for all the patterns. The cards in this book get increasingly more difficult. Therefore, start at the beginning. You will notice that you quickly get used to the technique of iris folding.

Preparation

1. Lay the card (13.8 x 9.5 cm) down with the back facing towards you.
2. Draw two pencil lines through the middle of the card. These lines will help you determine the place for your pattern.
3. Copy the basic square pattern 1 from this book
4. Place this model on the card using the lines which you drew earlier.
5. Use a pin to prick through the pattern and the card in the four corners.
6. Remove the pattern and carefully cut the square out of the card.
7. Tape the basic square pattern 1 to your cutting mat.
8. Place the card on top with the hole exactly over the pattern (you should be looking at the back of the card) and stick the top and bottom edges to your cutting mat using a couple of pieces of masking tape.
9. Choose four envelopes with different patterns. Four different beige and yellow envelopes have been used for the card shown in the top right-hand corner.
10. Cut 3 cm wide strips from these envelopes (either

1. The choice of colours: the inside of different envelopes.

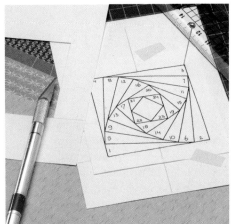

2. Copy the pattern onto the back of the card. Cut out the square.

3. Cut the envelopes into strips and fold them down. Stick the pattern to your cutting mat and place the card on top of it.

4. Place the strips exactly against the line and stick down the left-hand and right-hand sides using adhesive tape.

lengthways or widthways) and make separate
piles of colour A, colour B, colour C and colour D.

11. For each strip, fold a border (approximately 7 mm)
along the entire length with the _nice side_ facing
outwards.

IRIS folding

12. Take a folded strip of colour A and place this over
section 1, exactly against the line of the pattern with
the folded side facing _towards the middle_. Allow
1 cm to stick out on the left-hand and right-hand
sides and cut the rest away. By doing so, the strip will
also slightly stick out over the edge of the pattern at
the bottom, so that section 1 is totally covered.

13. Stick the strip to the card on the left-hand and
right-hand sides using a small piece of adhesive
tape, but remain 0.5 cm from the side of the card.

14. Take a strip of colour B and place it on section 2
on the pattern. Also tape this to the left-hand and
right-hand sides of the card.

15. Take a strip of colour C. Place this on section 3
and stick it into place.

16. Take a strip of colour D. Place this on section 4
and stick it into place.

17. You have now gone all the way around. Start again
with colour A on section 5, colour B on section 6,
colour C on section 7 and colour D on section 8.
Continue going round the card. The strips on sections
1, 5, 9, 13, 17 and 21 of this pattern are all of colour A.
The strips on sections 2, 6, 10, 14, 18 and 22 are all of
colour B. The strips on sections 3, 7, 11, 15, 19 and 23
are all of colour C. The strips on sections 4, 8, 12, 16,
20 and 24 are all of colour D.

Finishing

After section 24, carefully remove the card and
look at what you have made. Stick a single piece
of gold holographic paper in the middle on the
back of the card. Stick small pieces of double-
sided adhesive tape along the borders. Remove
the protective layer and fix your design on a
double card. Do not use glue, because all the
paper strips place pressure on the card. You can
also use punches, figure scissors, stickers, etc.
to add extra finishing touches to the card. To cut
the card using figure scissors, a pencil line is
drawn on the back of the card 0.5 cm from the
side. Cut along the line using the teeth of the
scissors. Fold the cut part backwards and carefully place the teeth of the scissors in the pattern
which has already been cut out. This will create a
border which continues in a smooth line.

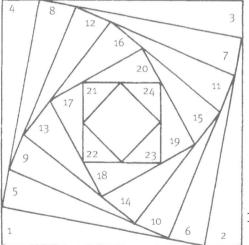

model 1

Materials

To make cards:
- Card (numbered colours are from Papicolor)
- Cutting knife
- Cutting mat
- Pencil
- Ruler with metal cutting edge (Securit)
- Adhesive tape
- Double-sided adhesive tape
- Masking tape
- Various punches (Tom Tas)
- Star hand punch (Fiskars)
- Hole punch
- Scissors and silhouette scissors
- Figure scissors (Fiskars)
- Ridge master
- Circle cutter
- Fine-liners
- Gel pens
- Photo glue
- Bobbles
- Sticker sheets
- Embossing pen
- Various embossing stencils
- Light box

IRIS folding
- Strips of used envelopes
- Green and blue IRIS folding text sheets
- Holographic paper

The middle
- Various colours of holographic paper
- Shiny origami paper

The patterns:
Full-size examples of all the patterns are given in this book. Copy them using a light box. The many straight lines make the patterns easy to cut out from the card. Useful aids for copying the patterns onto the card are the transparent plastic IRIS folding and drawing templates. These A5-size templates each have two different patterns. Specially punched cards are available for the candle, Christmas bell, Christmas tree and double star.

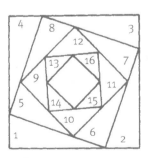

pattern 2

¹/₂ bow

Squares

Make the square cards according to the instructions given for the basis square.

Card 1

Card: Christmas red no. 43 (14.8 x 21 cm), olive green no. 45 (13.5 x 9.5 cm) and carnation white no. 03 (12.2 x 9 cm) • Pattern 1 • 3 cm wide strips from 4 different red and beige envelopes • Bronze gel pen • Bronze-green embroidery silk • Bronze holographic paper
Thread the embroidery silk around the square.

Card 2

Card: green (14.8 x 21 cm), light green (13.9 x 10 cm) and white (12.3 x 9.7 cm) • Pattern 1 • 3 cm wide strips from 4 different green envelopes • Holly corner punch • Gold holographic paper
Punch out the two top corners.

Card 3

Card: white (14.8 x 21 cm and 14.6 x 10.3 cm) • Pattern 1 • 3 cm wide strips from 4 different beige and brown envelopes • Gold holographic paper with stars • Gold thread
Attach the gold thread using photo glue.

3.

Card 4

Card: natural (14.8 x 21 cm) and yellow rainbow paper (13.8 x 9.5 cm) • Pattern 1 • 3 cm wide strips from 4 different yellow and beige envelopes • Diamond corner punch • Gold holographic paper

Cut the square out of the rainbow card. Punch out the corners and connect the corners using bronze lines.

Card 5

Card: white (14.8 x 21 cm and 14.6 x 10.3 cm) • Pattern 1 • 3 cm wide strips from 4 different red envelopes • Red holographic paper

Draw the half bow (page 7), fold it double along the dotted line and cut it out.

Card 6

Card: Christmas red no. 43 (14.8 x 21 cm) and white (14.2 x 9.9 cm) • Pattern 1 • 3 cm wide strips from 3 different red and green envelopes • Green "Merry Christmas" text strips • Gold holographic paper with stars

Finish this card with a box (3 x 4 cm) cut out of envelope paper. Attach the text strip's label using cotton.

6.

Make accompanying labels with pattern 2.

5.

Playing with squares

Glued stars and ice-crystals.

General information
The points for the star and the ice-crystal are made the same size by drawing a point on a wide strip of paper. Next, fold the strip double twice like a harmonica, staple it together and then cut out this point through the four layers. Cards 1, 3, 4 and 6: point a; card 5: points b and c; cards 2 and 7: point d.

Card 1
Card: violet no. 20 (14.8 x 21 cm and 14.6 x 10.3 cm) • Pattern 1 • 3 cm wide strips from 4 different blue envelopes • Silver holographic paper
Fold the card double and open it again. Draw pencil lines on the left-hand inner half through the middle. Place pattern 3 over the lines and prick all four holes. Cut out the square and finish the card off according to the instructions given in the basic techniques.

Card 2
Card: violet no. 20 (13.3 x 26.6 cm) and white (11.9 x 11.9 cm) • Pattern 3 • 2 cm wide strips from 4 different blue envelopes • Silver holographic paper • Star corner punch • Dark blue gel pen

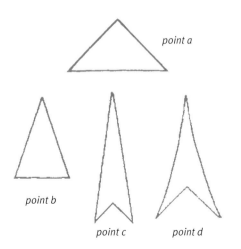

point a

point b

point c

point d

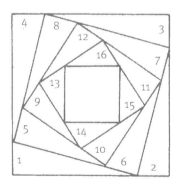

pattern 3

Punch out the corners of the white card. Cut a 12 x 5 cm strip of holographic paper and make the ice-crystal points. Decorate with lines using the gel pen.

Card 3

Card: iris blue no. 31 (14.8 x 21 cm and 14.6 x 10.3 cm) • Pattern 1 • 3 cm wide strips from 4 different used blue and grey envelopes • Silver holographic paper • Star punch

Card 4

Card: white no. 30 (14.8 x 21 cm and 14.6 x 10.3 cm) • Pattern 1 • 3 cm wide strips from 3 different lilac and red envelopes • White and blue text strips • Silver holographic paper • Silver gel pen

Card 5

Card: lilac no. 14 (13.3 x 26.6 cm) and lavender no. 21 (12.8 x 12.8 cm) • Pattern 3 • 2 cm wide strips from 3 different plain blue envelopes • Blue text strips • Silver holographic paper with stars • Geometric embossing stencil (Avec)

First, emboss the corners using the template's inner square. Cut the holographic paper to a size of 10 x 5 cm and 10 x 3.5 cm for the big and small points.

Card 6

Card: white (14.8 x 21 cm and 14.6 x 10.3 cm) • Pattern 1 • 3 cm wide strips from 2 red and 2 grey used envelopes • Silver holographic paper • Geometric embossing stencil

First, emboss the corners and cut the holographic paper to a size of 10 x 4 cm for the points.

Card 7

Card: lavender no. 21 (13.3 x 26.6 cm) and iris blue no. 31 (12.3 x 12.3 cm) • Pattern 3 • 2 cm wide strips from 4 different grey used envelopes • Silver holographic paper • Star corner punch • Star punch

First, punch out the corners of the iris blue card. Cut a 12 x 5 cm strip of holographic paper for the points.

Embossing

Place the embossing stencil on the good side of your card. Stick it in place using non-permanent adhesive tape. Fold the card open and place it (with the stencil) upside down on the light box. Carefully push the paper through the opening in the stencil using the embossing tool. You only have to push along the edge to raise the entire image.

Candles

Creating light in the dark

winter months.

Card 1

Card: Christmas green no. 18 (14.8 x 21 cm and 14 x 9.7 cm) and white (14.4 x 10.1 cm) • Pattern 4 with flame A • 3 cm wide strips from 3 different green envelopes • Green text strips • Gold holographic paper • Sticker lines and stars

Copy the pattern onto the back of the white card and cut out the candle and the flame. Fill the hole of the candle with strips of envelope paper. Fill the flame with strips of holographic paper. Cut a 12.5 x 7.8 cm square out of the front of the green card. Stick the white card on the inside against the square using double-sided adhesive tape.

Cover it with the green card.

Card 2

Card: night blue no. 41 (14.8 x 21 cm), iris blue no. 31 (13.3 x 9.5 cm) and white (13.5 x 9.1 cm) • Pattern 4 with flame B • 3 cm wide strips from 3 different blue envelopes • Blue text strips • Silver holographic paper with stars • Ornamental corner punch

Card 3

Card: Christmas red no. 43 (14.8 x 21 cm) and white (13.7 x 9 cm) • Pattern 4 with flame A • 3 cm wide strips from 4 different grey and red envelopes • Silver holographic paper • Star corner punch

Card 1a

Card: carnation white no. 03 (7 x 11 cm, and 6.8 x 5.3 cm) • Pattern 5 • 2 cm wide strips from 4 different red envelopes • Red holographic paper • Ice-crystal from a corner punch

Only cut out the candle. Fill the hole with strips. Cut the flame out of envelope paper and holographic paper. Stick the flame above the candle.

Tip: try using deco tape for the flame.

Card 2a

Card: white (7 x 11 cm, and 6.8 x 5.3 cm) • Pattern 5 • 2 cm wide strips from 4 different blue envelopes • Silver holographic paper with stars • Blue gel pen

Card 3a

Card: Christmas red no. 43 (7 x 11 cm, and 6.8 x 5.3 cm) • Pattern 5 • 2 cm wide strips from 4 different grey and red envelopes • Silver holographic paper • Silver gel pen

Christmas bells

To the left and right

Let them ring out!

Card 1

Card: night blue no. 41 (14.8 x 21 cm) and lavender no. 21 (13 x 9.2 cm) • Pattern 6 • 2.5 cm wide strips from 4 different blue envelopes • Silver holographic paper • Embossing stencil (Linda Design)
Emboss the text on the lavender card. Cut out the shape (note: not the tongue or the suspension eye!). Finish the card as described in the basic technique. Cut out the tongue and the suspension eye from envelope paper and stick them onto the card.

Card 2

Card: Christmas red no. 43 (14.8 x 21 cm) • Silver holographic paper (14.1 x 10.1 cm) and iris blue holographic paper no. 31 (13.7 x 9.8 cm) • Pattern 7 •

2.5 cm wide strips from 3 different light blue envelopes • White and blue text strips • Silver holographic paper • Comet embossing stencil (Linda Design) • Star punch
First, emboss (see page 11) the comet and 2 stars, and then stick the punched out white stars on the card.

pattern 4

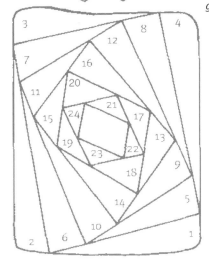

Card 3

Card: carnation white no. 03 (14.8 x 21 cm) and violet no. 20 (11.6 x 7.9 cm) • Pattern 7 • 2.5 cm wide strips from 4 different blue envelopes • Silver holographic paper • Holly embossing stencil (Linda Design)
Emboss the top right-hand corner of the white card. Round off the top right-hand corner of the violet card.

Card 4

Card: night blue no. 41 (14.8 x 21 cm) and carnation white no. 03 (13.8 x 9.5 cm) • Pattern 7 • 2.5 cm wide strips from 4 different used blue envelopes • Silver holographic paper with stars • Silver gel pen • Holly corner punch

Card 5

*Card: carnation white no. 03 (14.8 x 21 cm), iris
blue no. 31 (12.3 x 9.6 cm) and lavender no. 21
(10.5 x 8.7 cm) • Pattern 6 • 2.5 cm wide strips
from 4 blue different envelopes • Silver holographic
paper • Text sticker • Star punch*
Round off the corners of all the cards.

Card 6

*Card: night blue no. 41 (14.8 x 21 cm), silver holo-
graphic paper (14.2 x 10 cm) and carnation white
no. 03 (13.8 x 9.5 cm) • Pattern 6 • 2.5 cm wide
strips from 3 different blue envelopes • Blue text
strips • Silver holographic paper • Corner punch*
Punch out the corners of the white card.

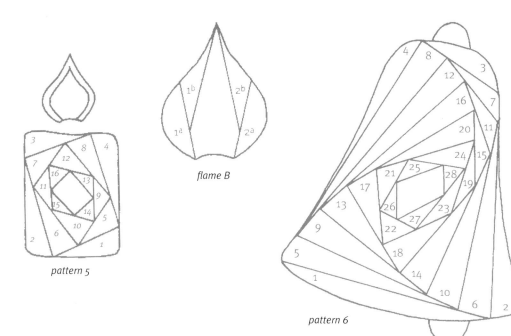

flame B

pattern 5

pattern 6

Christmas balls

It isn't Christmas without

these decorations!

Card 1

Card: Christmas red no. 43 (13.3 x 26.6 cm) and white (11.8 x 11.8 cm) • Pattern 8 • 3 cm wide strips from 2 red and 3 grey envelopes • Silver holographic paper • Holly corner punch

Punch out the corners of the white card. Cut out the Ø 7.5 cm circle slightly below the centre point (because of the suspension eye). Fill the ball according to the pattern. Copy the shape of the half suspension eye (see page 23) onto the holographic paper. Next, fold it double over the dotted line. Cut it out and stick it above the Christmas ball.

Card 2

Card: Christmas green no. 18 (13.3 x 26.6 cm) and white (10.7 x 10.7 cm) • Pattern 8 • 3 cm wide strips from 5 different green envelopes • Silver holographic paper for the small strips and the middle • Shell figure scissors

Cut decorative borders around the white card. Cut out the Ø 7.5 cm circle slightly below the middle point. Cut out 1 cm wide strips from the holographic paper. To make a nice fold line, score the back using a ruler and a pin. Add these small strips to colour B for sections 2, 7, 12, etc. This means that you must place a strip of colour B against the dotted line of section 2 and stick it in place. Place a small strip of holographic paper over the top of it against the continuous line of section 2 and stick it in place.

Continue with the other colours in sections 3, 4, 5 and 6. For section 7, place another strip of colour B against the dotted line and then place another small strip of holographic paper against the continuous line, etc. At the end, stick the finished design on the double green card.

Make a suspension eye as described for card 1.

Card 3

Card: dark green (13.3 x 26.6 cm and 11.2 x 11.2) and white (12.6 x 12.6 cm) • Pattern 8 • 3 cm wide strips from 4 different aquamarine envelopes • Gold holographic paper • Green text strips

Cut out the Ø 7.5 cm circle slightly below the centre of the white card.

Cut out 1 cm wide strips from gold holographic paper and add them to colour E in sections 5, 10, 15, etc. as described for card 2.

Make a suspension eye as described for card 1 and stick it above the Christmas ball together

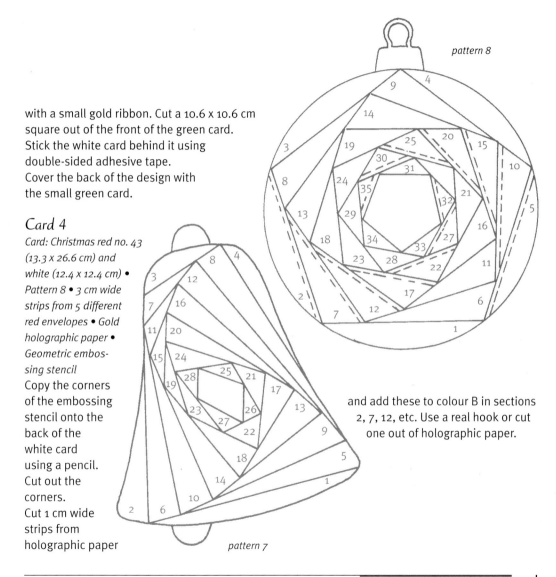

with a small gold ribbon. Cut a 10.6 x 10.6 cm
square out of the front of the green card.
Stick the white card behind it using
double-sided adhesive tape.
Cover the back of the design with
the small green card.

Card 4

Card: Christmas red no. 43
(13.3 x 26.6 cm) and
white (12.4 x 12.4 cm) •
Pattern 8 • 3 cm wide
strips from 5 different
red envelopes • Gold
holographic paper •
Geometric embos-
sing stencil
Copy the corners
of the embossing
stencil onto the
back of the
white card
using a pencil.
Cut out the
corners.
Cut 1 cm wide
strips from
holographic paper

and add these to colour B in sections
2, 7, 12, etc. Use a real hook or cut
one out of holographic paper.

pattern 8

pattern 7

Bookmarkers and labels

Bookmarker 1
Card: lavender no. 21 (21 x 6 cm) and Christmas green no. 18 (20 x 5.6 cm) • Pattern 9 • 1.5 cm wide strips from 5 different grey envelopes • Silver holographic paper • Ice-crystal corner punch

Bookmarker 2
Card: lavender no. 21 (21 x 6 cm) and night blue no. 41 (20 x 5.7 cm) • Pattern 2 • 2 cm wide strips from scrap pieces of grey and red envelopes • Silver holographic paper

Bookmarker 3
Card: snow-white no. 30 (21 x 6 cm) and violet no. 20 (20 x 5.7 cm) • Pattern 2 • 2 cm wide strips from scrap pieces of blue envelopes • Silver holographic paper

Bookmarker 4
Card: carnation white no. 03 (21 x 6 cm) and Christmas red no. 43 (20 x 6 cm) • Pattern 9 • 1.5 cm wide strips from 5 different beige envelopes • Gold holographic paper • Shell figure scissors

Card 1a
Card: white (7 x 11 cm and 6.8 x 5.3 cm) • Pattern 10 • 2 cm wide strips from scrap pieces of 3 different red envelopes • Red holographic paper • Star embossing stencil

Only cut out the tree. Stick the pot underneath at the end.

Card 2a
Card: white (7 x 11 cm) and yellow (6.8 x 5.3 cm) • Pattern 5 • 2 cm wide strips from 4 different red, orange and yellow envelopes • Gold holographic paper

Card 3a
Card: white (7 x 11 cm and 6.8 x 5.3 cm) • Pattern 10 • 2 cm wide strips from scrap pieces of 3 different green envelopes • Gold holographic paper • Star punch

Card 4a
Card: white (6 x 12 cm and 5.8 x 5.8 cm) • Pattern 9 • 1.5 cm wide strips from scrap pieces of 5 different green envelopes • Gold holographic paper • Holly corner punch

Card 5a
Card: white (7 x 11 cm and 6.8 x 5.3 cm) • Pattern 10 • 2 cm wide strips from scrap pieces of 3 different blue envelopes • Silver holographic paper • Star corner punch

Card 6a
Card: white (6 x 12 cm and 5.8 x 5.8 cm) • Pattern 9 • 1.5 cm wide strips from scrap pieces of 5 different red envelopes • Gold holographic paper • Flower corner punch • Red and gold gel pens

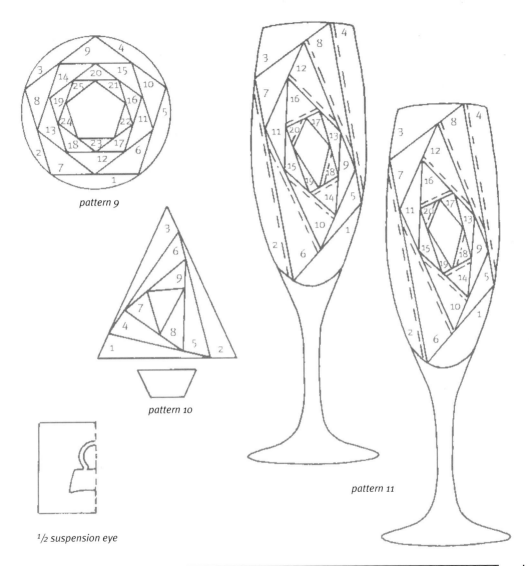

pattern 9

pattern 10

pattern 11

$^1/_2$ suspension eye

Champagne glasses

Cheers and best wishes

for the New Year!

Card 1

Card: night blue no. 41 (21 x 10.5 cm), caramel no. 26 (19.3 x 9.8 cm) and carnation white no. 03 (18.9 x 9.4 cm) • Pattern 11 • 2.5 cm wide strips from 4 different yellow, beige and green envelopes • 1 cm wide strips of gold holographic paper • Gold holographic paper • Hole punch

Cut out the tops of the glasses from the white card and fill them with strips. Note: add the narrow strips of holographic paper to colour D as follows. Cover section 1 with strips of colour A, section 2 with strips of colour B and section 3 with strips of colour C. Next, place a strip of colour D against the dotted line of section 4 and stick it in place.

Place a narrow strip of holographic paper over this against the continuous line of section 4 (see Christmas balls, card 2).

Continue round and add a narrow strip of holographic paper in sections 8, 12, etc. Cut out two stems at the same time from a piece of double-folded envelope paper and stick these on the card.

Card 2

Card: cream no. 03 (21 x 10.5 cm) and wine red no. 36 (19.3 x 9.7 cm) • Pattern 11 • 2.5 cm wide strips from 4 different beige and yellow envelopes • 1 cm wide strips of gold holographic paper • Gold holographic paper • Hole punch

Cut out the tops of the glasses from the wine red card. Note: add the narrow strips of holographic paper to colour B in sections 2, 6, 10, etc. according to the instructions given for card 1.

Card 3

Card: nut brown no. 39 (21 x 10.5 cm) and carnation white no. 03 (19.1 x 9.5 cm) • Pattern 11 • 2.5 cm wide strips from 4 different grey, beige and yellow envelopes • 1 cm wide strips of gold holographic paper • Gold holographic paper • Bronze gel pen • Hole punch

Add the strips of holographic paper to colour B in sections 2, 6, 10, etc. according to the instructions given for card 1.

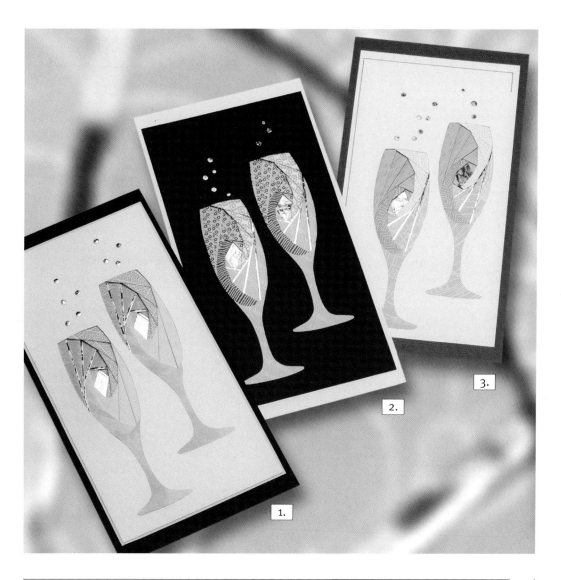

Christmas tree and double star

What would a Christmas card

be without a Christmas tree?

Card 1

*Card: carnation white no. 03 (14.8 x 21 cm),
red (13.8 x 9.5 cm) and raven black no. 01
(13. x 8.7 cm)* • *Pattern 12* • *2 cm wide
strips from 2 grey envelopes and 1 white
envelope* • *Silver holographic paper* •
Star corner punch

First, cut out a 3 mm strip from
both sides of the red card and
stick it on the card with a
1 mm gap to the left and to
the right of the red card.

Card 2

*Card: dark green (14.8 x
21 cm), gold (13.6 x
9.7 cm) and white (13.2
x 9.2 cm)* • *Pattern 12*
• *2 cm wide strips from 2 different
green envelopes* • *Green text strips*

Card 3

Card: carnation white no. 03 (14.8 x 21 cm)

and raven black no. 01 (13.8 x 9.5 cm) • *Holographic
card (14.1 x 9.8 cm)* • *Pattern 12* • *2 cm wide strips
from 2 different blue envelopes* • *White with blue
text strips* • *Star corner punch*

Punch out the corners of the holographic
card. Punch out the corners of the black
card and cut the stars out.

Card 4

*Card: white no. 30 (14.8 x 21 cm), gold
(14.8 x 10.5 cm) and green no. 18 (14.8 x
9.3 cm)* • *Pattern 12* • *2 cm wide strips
from 2 different green envelopes* •
White with green text strips • *Gold
holographic paper* • *Ice-crystals
from a corner punch* • *Shell
figure scissors*

Loose stars and ice-
crystals punched out of
deco tape are easy to
stick on the card.

Card 5

*Card: Christmas green no. 18 (14.8 x
21 cm), red (14.3 x 9.5 cm) and white
(13.3 x 8.5 cm)* • *Pattern 12* • *2 cm wide
strips from 3 different red envelopes* •
Silver holographic paper • *Silhouette stars*

model 12

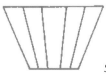

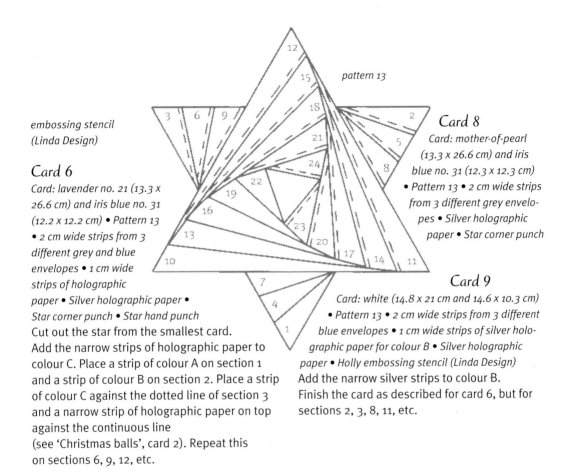

pattern 13

embossing stencil
(Linda Design)

Card 6

Card: lavender no. 21 (13.3 x
26.6 cm) and iris blue no. 31
(12.2 x 12.2 cm) • Pattern 13
• 2 cm wide strips from 3
different grey and blue
envelopes • 1 cm wide
strips of holographic
paper • Silver holographic paper •
Star corner punch • Star hand punch

Cut out the star from the smallest card.
Add the narrow strips of holographic paper to
colour C. Place a strip of colour A on section 1
and a strip of colour B on section 2. Place a strip
of colour C against the dotted line of section 3
and a narrow strip of holographic paper on top
against the continuous line
(see 'Christmas balls', card 2). Repeat this
on sections 6, 9, 12, etc.

Card 7

Card: red (14.8 x 21 cm) and mother-of-pearl
(13.4 x 9.6 cm) • Pattern 13 • 2 cm wide strips
from 2 grey envelopes and 1 red envelope • Silver
holographic paper • Geometric embossing stencil

Card 8

Card: mother-of-pearl
(13.3 x 26.6 cm) and iris
blue no. 31 (12.3 x 12.3 cm)
• Pattern 13 • 2 cm wide strips
from 3 different grey envelo-
pes • Silver holographic
paper • Star corner punch

Card 9

Card: white (14.8 x 21 cm and 14.6 x 10.3 cm)
• Pattern 13 • 2 cm wide strips from 3 different
blue envelopes • 1 cm wide strips of silver holo-
graphic paper for colour B • Silver holographic
paper • Holly embossing stencil (Linda Design)

Add the narrow silver strips to colour B.
Finish the card as described for card 6, but for
sections 2, 3, 8, 11, etc.

Woolly hat and jumper

Warmly dressed for winter.

Card 1

Card: purple no. 13 (14.8 x 21 cm) and white (12.5 x 8.6 cm) • Pattern 14 • 2.5 cm wide strips from orange, pink and purple envelopes • 2.5 x 8 cm strip of colour C • Gold holographic paper • Ice-crystal corner punch • Snow embossing stencil • Bobble

Cut the woolly hat out of the white card; be careful: do not cut the brim. Emboss the snow-flakes. Fill the shape. For the brim of the woolly hat, put the wide strip through the ridge master, cut out the shape and stick it to the card. Punch out the ice-crystals. Finally, stick the bobble onto the card.

Card 2

Card: aquamarine (14.8 x 21 cm), night blue no. 41 (13.5 x 9.5 cm) and carnation white no. 03 (12.5 x 8.6 cm) • Pattern 14 • 2.5 cm wide strips from 3 different purple and aquamarine envelopes • 2.5 x 8 cm strip of colour B • Rainbow holographic paper • Ice-crystal punch • Bobble

Card 3

Card: dark blue no. 41 (14.8 x 21 cm), pink (13.1 x 9.6 cm) and mother-of-pearl (13.6 x 9.1 cm) •

Pattern 15 • 3 cm wide strips from 4 different purple envelopes • Silver holographic paper • Star punch

Cut the body (not the sleeves) out of the mother-of-pearl card. Fill the hole with the strips. Copy the sleeves of the pattern onto the back of envelope paper (colour C). Cut them out and stick them next to the jumper.

Card 4

Card: olive green no. 45 (14.8 x 21 cm), aquamarine (14.1 x 10.1 cm), night blue no. 41 (13.4 x 9.8 cm) and white (13.2 x 9.1 cm) • Pattern 15 • 3 cm wide strips from 3 different green envelopes • Green text strips • Silver holographic paper • Ice-crystals from the corner punch

Card 5

Card: turquoise no. 32 (14.8 x 21 cm), night blue no. 41 (14 x 9.6 cm) and white (12.7 x 9.3 cm) • Pattern 14 • 2.5 cm wide strips from 3 different bright green envelopes • 2.5 x 8 cm strip of colour C • Silver holographic paper • Ice-crystal figure punch • Bobble

Cut the woolly hat and punch out the ice-crystals from the white card.

Card 6

Card: night blue no. 41 (14.8 x 21 cm) and carnation white no. 03 (13.3 x 9.7 cm) • Pattern 14 • 2.5 cm

wide strips from 3 different blue envelopes • 2.5 x
8 cm strip of colour C • Silver holographic paper •
Star corner punch • Snow embossing stencil
(Linda Design) • Bobble

Card 7

Card: purple no. 13 (14.8 x 21 cm) and white (13.7 x
9.2 cm) • Pattern 15 • 3 cm wide strips from 4
different purple, orange and red envelopes • Gold
holographic paper • Ice-crystal corner punch

Card 8

Card: white (14.8 x 21 cm and 14.6 x 10.3 cm) •
Pattern 15 • 3 cm wide strips from 4 different blue
envelopes • Silver holographic paper • Figure
scissors • Snow embossing stencil
Emboss the snowflakes (see page 11). Cut
the body out of the 'landscape' card. Cut the
sleeves from envelope paper (colour B). Cut
a decorative border along the bottom edge.
Fill the border with a strip which measures
2 x 14.8 cm (colour A). Cover the design.

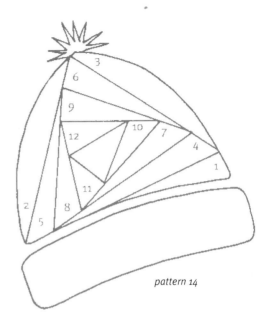

pattern 14

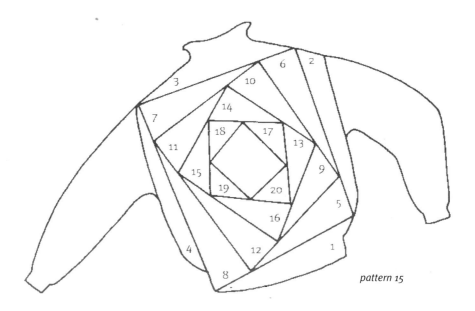

pattern 15

Thanks to:
Kars & Co BV, Ochten, the Netherlands
Papicolor, Utrecht, the Netherlands (card material)
CreaArt, Apeldoorn, the Netherlands
for providing the material.

The materials used can be ordered by shopkeepers from:
Avec B.V., Waalwijk, the Netherlands